Water fun

Bobbie Neate

The writing in this text is persuasive. This book is designed to make you think about the writing in advertisements.

The book is different to many other information books because the writing on each page is trying to persuade you that water is fun. Each chapter is about water and the things you can do with it. Each page encourages you to either buy, play or go to places which have or use water. One page persuades you that bath toys are the greatest fun while another page suggests that theme parks will give you the biggest thrills.

After you have read the text, you can decide whether water really is fun and, if you had the chance, which toy you would buy or which trip you would go on.

Do not read every page, just turn to the pages that interest you.

Contents

1 Water toys

Simple or more difficult, there are plenty of water toys.

Boats

Boats come in all different sizes but they are all fun. They can be blown by the wind or powered by motor. Whatever model you choose you will have fun with water and boats.

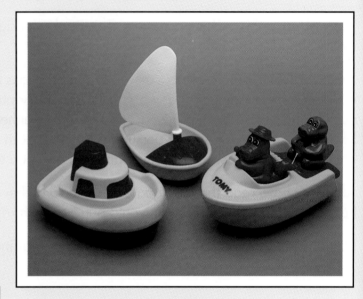

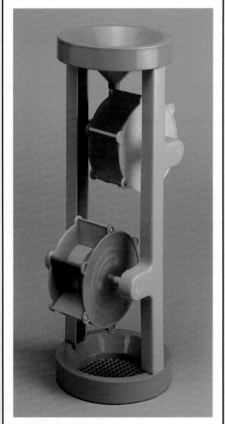

Water wheels

Have fun watching the water pour through the hole and sprinkle over the wheel. There are all sorts of games you can play with these wheels.

Canal play

This toy is for the beach or the garden. You can make a very simple canal or a really big and difficult one. It has a castle which has a giant water wheel, a lock with gates and a boat. Or perhaps you want to play with the harbour where the boats can be loaded with containers using the crane.

Water riders

What about a ride on this crocodile's back? No? Then what about a ride on a more friendly whale? Or perhaps you prefer the faster pace of a motorbike? Water riders can be made in all sorts of shapes. Whichever you choose, you can float and dangle your feet in the water. You are sure to have watery fun.

2 Water bombs

Cheap and simple but oh, what fun – a water bomb. Fill them up, make sure of your aim and throw. Everybody will get a soaking.

⬆ Bombs full of water and ready for action!

Like many water games, water bombs are more fun in the sun but some people find them thrilling whether it's hot or cold.

Just fill the thin balloon with water, find your mates and look out! You may get a wetting yourself …

Throw your bomb fast and with care. If you are lucky it will burst as it hits your pal. Look how wet everyone gets.

3 Rain and washing up

Rain

Perhaps the most simple pleasure of all is the pouring rain.

When the rain comes beating down, just dress up properly and out you go. No need for toys. Just feel the rain beat on your head or on your hand. Just feel the trickle of water as it reaches your tummy. It can be nice or it can be nasty. The simple pleasure of water from the sky.

Watering the garden is fun too. Who says helping in the garden is dull and boring? Oh no, when there's water around nothing is dull. Find a watering can and a hose and you will soon be happy, and helpful too.

Washing up

Have you ever noticed how much fun washing up can be? You can turn on the taps and watch the water flow. Let it bubble and gurgle through the colander as the water rushes through the tiny holes. Washing a mug can be fun. Let the water fall from a height and see the ripples below.

↑ Yes, washing dishes can be fun!

Warning

Do not waste water. Water is far too important to us all. Never think nobody will mind if you make a mess with water. They always will. **Too much water** can damage a house or garden.

4 Paddling pools

Paddling pools come in all shapes and sizes but
there will be one to please you. The sun is on
your back and you are all ready for action ...

Big pools

Big pools are big enough for you and your friends.

⬆ You can have fun splashing all your friends!

Small pools

Small pools are just big enough for you and you alone. No need to let anyone else play with your water toys.

Special pools

What about a pool with a slide? What fun to slide down into the water. Try this new one for size.

Warning

Never play in water on your own. Always make sure an adult is with you. You could slip and have an accident. Play safe!

5 Water guns

Everybody has fun with a water gun! Use it in the garden when the weather is hot.

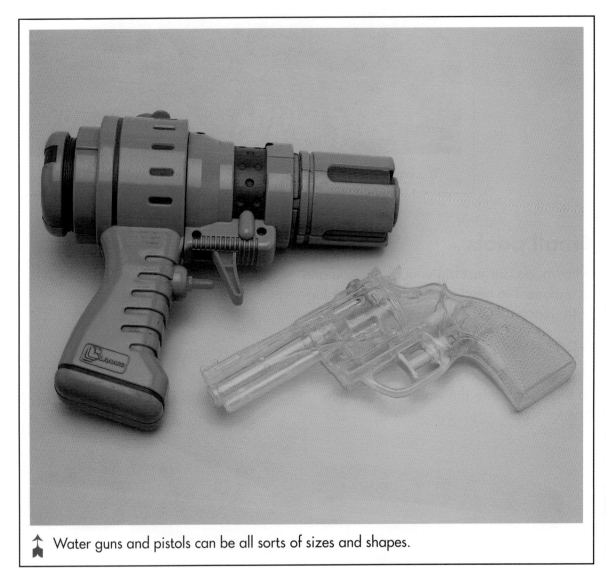

↑ Water guns and pistols can be all sorts of sizes and shapes.

Imagine a hot day. You are dressed for action and your friends come round. All you need is a bit of water fun to cool you down.

Squeeze the trigger and out comes loads of water to soak your friends. Which one will get the wettest?

A small water pistol can be hidden and used quickly when you need it. But a big air-pressure water gun gives you lots of extra power and you can hit people from metres away. If your aim is good, you will get your friends just where you want.

You can make your own water gun out of an old plastic bottle. Look at the book called *Water experiments*.

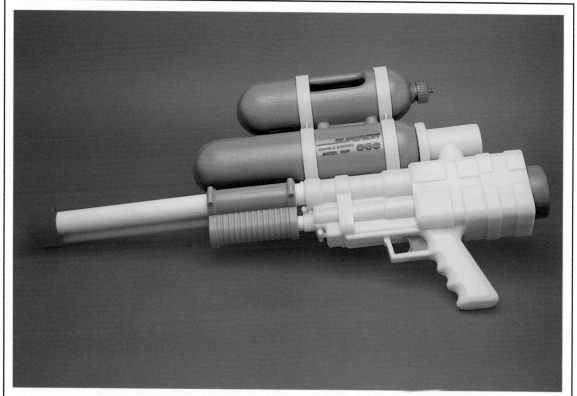

 The barrel holds lots of water, so you won't run out of water just when you need it most.

Warning

Do not shoot at anyone's eyes. Do not spray adults with water – people do not like being sprayed with water when they are not expecting it.

6 Bath toys

The best time of the day – bath time. The time to get clean and the time to play with those action-packed toys.

Which do you want to play with?

Bath time boat

You have got to get this boat. This toy is the most brilliant you can buy. It looks just like any other boat but just you wait to see what it can do.

First you float it in the bath. Then put teddy in the captain's seat. Pull the rope as hard as you can – and wait for action. The funnel spurts water – high like a fountain. Then, when you are not expecting it, out leaps teddy and lands in the water with a big

splash.

Water elephant

This is the best bath toy I have played with. I really never get tired of it.

Just sit the water elephant near your bath. Make sure his long tail is in the water, then squeeze his back and watch his nose! Out comes this brilliant jet of water to hit you smack on the nose or, better still, whoever is in the bath with you!

Activity toy

Now what about this toy?

It has all the actions. Enough to keep the whole family amused. It has a squirter, a tap, a water wheel and a scoop. And it hangs ready for action on the side of the bath.

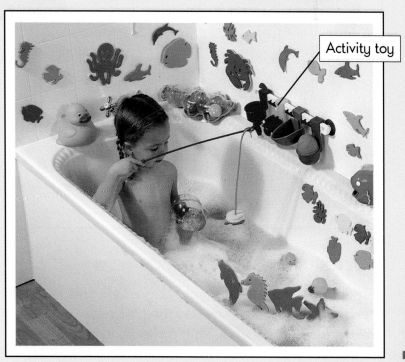

Activity toy

Whistling dolphin

Very simple and easy to use but it's a winner. Soak her, squeeze her but look out for her spurt! Watch her mouth and she will soak you. Just to add to her skills she whistles as she squirts. Play with her and you are sure to have fun.

Ducks

Perhaps you just want a simple play with a firm friend. Ducks never change and they are never dull. Get a classic yellow duck, with a cheeky face and red beak and you have found a real watery friend.

7 Swimming pools

Can you swim? Whether you can or not, you can have great fun in a pool. Big pools, small pools, leisure pools … Whichever you choose, you are sure to have a good time.

Shallow, warm pools

If you haven't learned to swim yet and you are not sure about the cold water, I am sure you will enjoy the warm water of this pool. Just splash around and have fun.

Big pools

Ever dreamed of swimming to an island? Well, you can swim a long way in this pool. It is the size of a large superstore and you will never be short of a friend. 850 people can all swim at the same time and still there's room for you.

Wave machines

Ever wanted to be at the sea but inside? Well, a wave machine can do just that! Just roll up to the edge of the pool and wait for the waves. Waves come along every half hour so it's never too long to wait for a bit of wave hopping.

Beach pools

Ever wanted to be at the beach but not wanted the journey to get there? Try this beach. It's miles from the sea but who cares? It has all the water you could wish for.

Indoor beaches

Perhaps you prefer a painted beach with plenty of sprinklers. In these pools you get wet from above as well as below.

⬆ Relax and enjoy a jacuzzi!

Jacuzzis

What about a soak as warm as can be? Get in this jacuzzi and you will never want to get out. Bubbles ... jets ... what else could you ask for?

8 Theme park water attractions

What about a day out at a theme park. Want to get wet? You will at a theme park. No doubt about that. But which one will you like best I wonder?

Will it be ...

... the Dinoboats

All aboard for the bumper ride of your life. Yes this is the water ride with a difference. It's dodgems on the water where you can safely race and chase each other in motorised rubber tubes. Bump or be bumped, it all adds to a whole lot of wet fun!

... Depth Charge

Take a deep breath before you sweep down the great water slide. Get into a raft, hold on tight and down you go. As you reach the bottom of this long trip wait for the puddles. They are sure to splash you and there is no chance of staying dry.

... Thunder River

Hold tight – a white-water rafting ride taking everyone for a spin. You splash through canyons and tunnels and waterfalls. Watch out for the jets of water ready to catch you when you are not expecting it. Getting wet is all part of the fun.

... Loggers Leap

Ever wanted to climb great heights in a canoe and then come crashing down into a pool of water? Ever wanted to get really wet? If so, this is the ride for you. Everyone can be together in this log-shaped canoe. Just sit tight and enjoy the view. Then down you come with a very big splash. And, oh boy, are you cool!

9 The seaside

Off on holiday for a week, down to the seaside. Oh, you lucky thing. Five glorious miles of sand with glistening warm water to play in. Days will be endless with all you have ever wanted from a holiday by the sea.

↑ Wish you were here!

If you feel like relaxing you could paddle in the shallow water, feel the cool water trickling over your feet and between your toes.

If you feel more adventurous you could try to jump the big waves as they come crashing in. Jump them, don't let them get you. Run out to the sea and then as soon as the next wave breaks run as fast as you can for the safety of the dry sand. However many times you play this game, the waves will get you in the end, with their salty smack behind the knees. Waves just love to pick on those little people (and bigger people) who think they are safe!

We don't want to go home.

Find a trickle of water down by the sea and play all sorts of games with a bucket and spade. Dams are the best. First, find the running water, then build the dam. Will your dam be strong enough to resist the incoming waves?

Part of the fun of the sea is to see it destroy the things you've built in the sand.

Water never loses its power to give you fun.

21

10 Water sports

Learn a sport and have even more fun with water.

Sailing

Sailing is the best. Feel the power of the wind pushing you along. Steering your boat and finding the wind gives you a great buzz.

⬆ You can learn in an Optimist dinghy.

Fishing

Fishing is cool. Watch those juicy fish just go for your line and hey presto! You have them for your dinner.

Surfing

Surfing – well, now there's sport. Get out that board, wait for the right wave and you are away. Away to the beach on the crest of a wave.

Some people learn to stand on their surf boards.

Rafting

Are you brave enough for the white-water rapids? Feel the wind in your face, and with an oar in your hand you are away, down past the most difficult rock. Go for it.

Further information

For more information about water read the book called *Water is a solid, liquid and gas*. If you want to experiment with water read *Water experiments* and if you want to know why it rains read *Reference book of water and weather*.